OUTWITTING GRAVITY

OUTWITTING GRAVITY

JOAN VAN POZNAK

POEMS

Published by Versed Impressions

West Palm Beach, Florida

www.versedimpressions.com

Cover copyright © Monika Beisner, "Daphne"
from Ovid's Metamorphoses

Back cover, Lawrence Holofcener, "Allies,"
The Philip Hulitar Sculpture Garden, Society of the Four Arts,
Palm Beach, Florida
Photograph, Frederick Van Poznak

Graphic design by Geraldine Aikman

For Elissa, Karen, Christopher, Nicholas,
Nigel and Frederick the Great

I've written you a poem

Every year you've been on earth,

As your Mother or Grandmother,

Sixty years I've been your Wife,

Twenty something as a Muminlaw…

The inspiration's rife.

And there's no sign of it stopping,

Nor of the love and mirth,

Because you are the wellspring of my life.

CONTENTS
PART I

CONTENTS
PART II

PART ONE

SPLIT AFFINITIES

Poems 1970 – 1995

Antiquery

I love old books, old wine, old friends,
Old furniture and odds and ends,
Old clothes I welcome to the fold...
So why don't I love getting Old?

Viola d'Amore

"Woman is a delightful instrument, of which love is the bow and man the artist" ...Stendhal

She was his instrument, and oh,
How well he wielded love's bow.
At any hour, in any key,
He played with virtuosity.

But after years of harmony,
She started losing her esprit,
And then her bridge began to crack,
He lost a screw, his bow went slack.
Her F-holes warped, her belly swelled,
She creaked whenever she was held.
His fiddling became erratic,
His technique merely automatic.
Appassionata's soon gave way
To rallentandos, then, no play.

One day he placed her on the shelf,
And humming softly to himself,
Put on his coat and left, hell bent,
To find a better instrument.

Intimacy

Seamus is famous,
And oh, my pride,
We've lain together,
Side by side

No two could share
A closer space,
Than we, when pressing
Face to face.

And yet, we've never met.
Surprised?
It's how we've been
Anthologized. *

*Victorian Guitar by Seamus Heaney & Viola d'Amore
by Joan Van Poznak appeared side by side in:
Faber Book of Blue Verse, Faber & Faber, 1990
Making Love to Marilyn, Viking, 1997

Now and Zen

In Edo, the Floating World,
Kyoka held high status
For their crazy verse.

If I could span two hundred years
And join that comicazee gang,
I'd have to be a man
To make a rhyme...
Or a subversifying concubine.

Music Lover's Diet

"Love never dies of starvation, but often of indigestion."
...Ninon de Lenclos

"If music be the food of love, etc." ...William Shakespeare

A balanced meal of love's cuisine
Will leave us satisfied and lean.
A little portion, for a starter
Of Beethoven's "Appassionata,"
Then steaming soupçons of Suppé
To warm us for the roundelay.

The fish course next, perhaps we'll net
A freshly fiddled "Trout" Quintet,
Then, piece de resistance, bring on
A tender filet from "Mignon."

"Drink to me only with thine eyes"...
Then we won't have to Breathalyze,
And after, pet, our just dessert:
A gentle "Liebesliede" flirt.
To follow, pretty amorata,
A demi of "Coffee Cantata";
Then nightcaps before we've defrocked
Of good old "Eine Kleine Nacht..."
And just one chestnut for a treat,
So pass me the "Nutcracker," sweet.

There, soup to nuts, yet no suggestion,
No tiny hint of indigestion.
So, darling, let's put out the light.
"My head is splitting...not tonight!"

5

On Seeing Gavin Ewart in Sainsbury's

It must be the Muses day off,
And poets also eat.
So down from lofty heights into the street
The shopping list: more grapes and pomegranates?
Try finding nectar here on Putney High.
Can you imagine Swinburne
Emerging from The Pines
To purchase tins of beans
By Messrs Heinz?
Or Eliot…he dared to eat a peach,
But buy them? Fortnum's maybe,
Or on some Aegean beach.
Not on the Costa Putney
Where the natives quench their gluttony
To ritual choreography
In the brightly lit monotony
Of Sainsbury's.

Outside, the rhythm section of endless traffic furies,
Perfumes of a thousand and one lorries,
Inhabitants, pale and lumpy, rush and jostle,
Expressions blank, some friendly, some looking hostile.
Do they know of greener grasses
Than this grey ground of the working classes?

And here's our local poet
Leaning on a wire trolley.
Perhaps it's just a decoy
While he observes the pageant of Man's Folly,
Stocks up on food for thought.
He watched it all,
I looked twice, caught his eye.
Was that returning glance a Poet's
Or mere curiosity?
I've read his dirty stuff…
My chicken and I hurried by,
Returned to cook the stew.
Did he go home and write a poem too?

Love Portions

"Of all heavy bodies, the heaviest is the woman we have ceased to love." ...Lemontey

He left. Our love was on the rocks,
And I took to the chocolate box.
Depressed and utterly despondent
I fortified myself with fondant.
There's never been another man...
A bite or two of marzipan.
When passion play became passé,
Sweet solace was marron glacé.
And keeping me from misery,
A little French patisserie.
I'm haunted by a wistful tune,
I think it's called "Eclair de Lune."
Bereft I wander in a fog
Of strudel mit a bit of schlag.

When love descended to a plateau,
I never swallowed pride...just gateau.
He drove me to hi-cal dejection,
The object of all my confection.
And now love's gone, I'm overcome
With heavy heart and heavy bum.
If only he'd come back to stay,
I could exist on Perrier.

Another love? I'll never risk it...
Well...maybe after one more biscuit.

Excess Baggage

Carrying Teddy to bed,
Carrying school bags and skates,
Carrying notebooks and music
And lipstick on dates,
Carrying groceries and trays,
Caring and worrying,
Loving and marrying,
Carrying bridal bouquets,

Carrying credit cards, door keys
And car keys. Carrying babies,
Inside and outside.
Toys and more groceries.
Bags on vacation trips, guilty relationships,
Carrying good news and bad news,
Rumours, ill humours and duty free booze,
Carrying tunes in your head,
Unfinished knitting and books never read,
Carrying memories, shopping bags,
Shoes that need soles.
Bearing the burden and wearing the roles
Of Mother and Lover, of Wife and of Friend.
Faltering at every step.
So, what is life in the end?
You might say,
Carrying on
Until you're carried away.

Summer Flowers

Returning home, the room is alive
With vivid mementos of the last fortnight.
Floral calling cards, a serendipity
Of color joined by chance.

Alfred, the gardener, brings seasonal flourishes
Early every Friday morning.
Last week's roses are gone,
But the greenery lingers on,
Soft petals with a few yellow tiger lilies
Snarling for center stage.
Sylvia brought them over a week ago,
And since we've been to Lucerne together
Making music.

There are the remains of Barbara's presentation bouquet.
She came to sing Mozart at the Proms,
Flying off next morning, leaving me her blooms.
All pinks and blues, mums, carnations and white lilies,
Making an Exultate in the room.
Mingled in are still a few dark pink carnations
Brought by Grace and Ira, passing through
From Nice, where he plays every summer.

A medley of flowers, music,
Changing friends and linens.
Impromptu meals, good talk, wine, laughter.
No wonder, like the blossoms,
I'm wilting slightly, too.

Requiem for a Lost Glove

One glove
Lost off hand, out of pocket,
Somewhere between Putney Bridge Station,
And the rest of London, somehow.
Right hand, left as a token of my aberration,
Well worn and taken for granted
Until now.

I examine its mate, the left hand glove,
Admire the leather and the crocheted string,
Appreciate the hand stitching as I never did before.
I never thought a thing about them as a pair.
Now one's not there and I'm in mourning
For the late departed mate.

Who'd think you'd need to wear gloves June, the First?
But going to a lunchtime concert at St. Giles,
Cripplegate...
Ah! Could I have dropped it there? No. The Vicar said
Their Verger looked with care.

Can you believe the news at Baker Street?
The Lost and Found says not one glove
Was turned in June, the First or Second.
It's obvious I'm out of season, out of fashion,
And unreasonably obsessed
With one small dispossession.

Old Hat

This black velvet beret
Your Mother made for mine
In 1940-something,
Has worn its way through three generations,
Jauntily, with your Mama's stylish label
Still intact:
created by helen goodman, (lower case),
I send it on a sentimental journey back,
To spend the next five decades at your place.

From New York to London to California…
The perfect traveling hat.
A velvet time capsule, always a la mode,
A touch bohemian in its day.
Making a small statement
As it sat aloft in Carnegie Hall,
Where I doubt it was asked to be doffed,
Since Mother and the hat were both quite small.

Abroad in the 50's to see the chapeau country;
In Greenwich Village, its natural habitat,
Then in the dress-up box, my girls
Felt so grown up in that black hat.
Out of the closet in the 60's…hip, hip, beret!
Slouched through the 70's, dashed past the 80's
Into premature retirement, saved for a rainy day.

If there's a Millinery Academy Hall of Fame,
That's where it deserves to rest...unless
It carries on with all your progeny.
Full circle, each stitched segment like
A portion of our lives,
Not all a piece of cake, but circles never stop.
This is a classic case, to be continued
On a new head and shining face.

For Dorothy Demke

Found

In the bottom,
At the back
Of a desk drawer

Frayed and faded,
In a box with no lid,
Is a ticket that says:

KEEP THIS TICKET.

So I did.

Notice on the door of a Council house in Battersea:

No Hawkers

No Canvassers

No Junk Mail

And Especially

No Jehovah's Witnesses.

Comparative Religion, West Palm Beach, Florida (Circa 1990)

There are many roads to God,
And two of them are in our neighborhood.
Dixie Highway, byway to Heaven,
And Broadway (not the Great White Way),
Surely a path to righteousness.
At least it's the right track to all that's good.

No great cathedrals here,
These are the storefront congregations,
And in a nation born to shop, it isn't odd
To shop for God.

In the beginning, you might start at
The Gate of Heaven Church of Our Lord of Apostolic Faith, Inc.,
Or if that's too much to tackle,
Follow the road to **The Street Called Straight Tabernacle**,
Where they tell it like it is.
The Upper Room of Jesus Christ Written in Heaven,
Is on street level, so, walk right in,
And at **The True Faith Revival Church,** Bishop H.H.
Norman, Pastor,
Is stamping out sin.
Tucked in between **Nettie's Alterations for Men and Women**
And **Atlantic Menu Signs**, there are signs, the Pastor sayeth,
That all men, women and children could be altered
if they found true faith.

**The New Evergreen Missionary Baptist & First
Tabernacle of Jesus Christ**,
(Next to **The Good Stuff** thrift shop)
Has God's good stuff in store.
So has **The Crown of Glory Church of God in Christ**,
**Teaching the Unreached
Pentecostal Deliverance**, where they preach
Some points that others might not reach.
**The Church of God, The Profit and The Church of
God of Prophesy**
May split hairs, while
The Supernatural Church of God
Could be the answer to your prayers.

Tired of shopping?
Hop on the baby blue bus that says:
Apostle J.T. Campbell & The Deliverance Team,
And hear the gospel while you stop
At every station on the crossroad to salvation.

Mother Funk

I'm a post-impressionist, self-expressionist,
True confessionist Woman.
I've got more than one string to my ham. I am
The degeneration gap,
Pre-shrunk, post-punk
Seminal derivator of
Mother Funk.

I'm a Spock 'n role, Stockin' roll Mama.
I've got low expectations of all relations
That make high drama.
Got the valium-yums, got the shrinks and the kinks,
All that flab and the mini pants
Menopause renaissance junk.
I've got Mother Funk.

I was the pre-pill pillar of the whole megillah
Read novels, dieted, while hot beds rioted,
What did I get? Nyet.
Angst for the mammeries,
Consultant Samurai's took a chunk.
Then I heard reveille, got myself heavily
Into Mother Funk.

Want to bust the cage, find the Fountain of Middle Age,
Spread ugly roomers, transplant sense of humours,
Grow a mustache, Flash!
Draw my perimeters, immature similars
Need not apply until I
Grab my hunk
Of Mother Funk.

I'm an existentialist with a shopping list,
Post-partumultuous creature.
A double-breasted double feature,
One-woman rhythm band…parenthood wasn't planned,
Jives to the pipes of a different plumber,
Sings 'til I'm sunk
In Mother Funk.

I may flunk the means test, the old baggy jeans test
Won't darken my Dior. The poor are so pure.
I'm slumming down market and love it, I'll lark it.
This mission's position is: Ma's on top.
Mama cop rules in this bunk…
It's all Mother Funk.

I'm a fully gendered, single entendréd,
Open-ended Ms.
Haven't forgotten what I've begotten, which is,
Daughters, reporters of current affairs.
Their poor old Dad thinks the harem's gone mad,
And while he says his prayers,
I'm power drunk
On Mother Funk.

Euro-Squawk

As even little children know,
All proper Yankee roosters crow
A classic "cock-a-doodle-doo,"
There's nothing you can misconstrue.

Yet Europeans all agree
The lyrics go: "ki-ki-ri-ki"...
Though chickens don't change one iota
From Sicily to North Dakota.

If fowl talk is the subject of such wide interpretation,
It's frightening to think what else gets cocked-up in
translation.

Life Lines

Madame de Sevigné said, and I quote:
"The heart has no wrinkles." …and fingered her throat.
But Monsieur Sarrasin, a so-called French wit,
Wrote: "Wrinkles are love's grave," the old hypocrite.

So you may feel young as a newly sprung lamb,
But with epidermis that's puckered, Madame,
Though your heart is as smooth as kid gloves,
Think of bidding adieu to your loves.

On the other hand, Shakespeare, our rational Will,
Penned: "Age cannot wither her," twirling his quill,
While another French scholar, Boileau, wrote, "Each age
Contains its own pleasures," and winked at the page.

So it seems, Sarrassin, great minds disagree,
de Sevigne, Shakespeare, Boileau…to name three.
Let the creases increase, just as long as you're blessed
With a fellow who sees that your wrinkles get pressed.

Split Affinities

Neither here nor there,
It's curious that elements as nebulous as air,
As ill defined as space,
Should make this solid mass, this body
So displaced.

One entity, two lives, divided by an ocean,
Suspended animation and beliefs,
Trapped somewhere in the time
That's lost or gained,
Compressed into the hours that remain.

In the muted London night,
My head sinks into pillows,
My mind a continent away.
Sleep doesn't come. I make a cup of tea,
Stare out the window, drinking in my hydrotherapy:
The tranquilizing Thames.
Ink black, slow motion with reflecting lights.
Silence. Then one bird sings.

Tomorrow night will be more restless still.
New York, where concrete screams,
Alarms, emergencies harangue,
Intruding on drugged dreams
Of high achievers while they sleep.
Letting cacophonies compete.

The involuntary inner clock,
Instinctive as the crowing cock,
An out of joint
Circadian counterpoint.
Which pill will fix the loose connection
In my biologic rhythm section?

A daughter on each continent,
And half a mind in each.
The heart expands as far as it can reach,
But part of me dissolves into the air.
How vital are those missing hours, unspent,
When I am neither here nor there.

Side Effects

I'm worried about too much Yoga.
Just what will I get for my pains?
If I stand on my head every morning,
I might end up with varicose brains.

Febulous

Febrile February, a month to yearn
For any other month, and to concern
Ourselves with temperatures as they're conveyed
In Celsius, in Fahrenheit and Centigrade.

Lackluster, lacking lust and all desire.
Instead, corroding throat, temples of fire,
Echoing coughs, chilblains and woolly vests,
Along with germs are my unwelcome guests.

I've caught the lot, but I missed Cupid's barb,
For Valentine, that sinner in saint's garb,
Has turned to frog my erstwhile charming prince…
No wonder February makes me wince.

But, as the heartless month moves bleakly on,
If I remember the phenomenon,
One consolation may restore my zest:
This damn month's that much shorter than the rest.

A Little Yeyekatualiruru* in the Garden

It's too hot in this new wave heat wave
For big talk.
We will discuss philosophy and politics
When the sun goes down.

Now we sit beneath the most promising tree,
Waiting for a breeze,
Mind and body separate as any guru's,
Exchanging lazy Yeyekatualirurus.

* small talk of the Yawalapiti Indians of Brazil's Upper Xingu

A Conversazione
December 4,1980, *The London Times*

I was fascinated to read in the *Times*
That the Duke of Edinburgh was present at a
conversazione
At the Royal Society of Arts yesterday.

That's quite a coincidence,
Because I've just returned from one myself.
As a matter of fact, hardly a day goes by
That a conversazione isn't being thrown by someone in
my set.
And while we're not about to run out of respirazione,
I'm looking for a new way of entertaining…or
Throwing a little receptzione down my way.

It seems to me it's time.
To revive the Levee (formerly Levy?)
And combined with the conversazione,
It might liven up the social scenario considerably.

Think of it, sipping cafe au lait in a smart negligee
Under the duvet while the champagne cools in the bidet…
And settle the affairs of the day…
What to wear, where to play…how you say…
Isn't it an inspirazione?

(Or am I full of baloney?)

Big Sur, The Magic Mountain

There is a window to the sky
In Danny's house. You lie in bed
And watch so many stars
It makes you funny in the head.

And if they're fighting for their lives,
The view from here appears to be
That their congested universe
Is a sea of tranquility.

Transfixed, you watch the moon appear,
At once attracting center stage,
Outshining all but a few stars
Who hang on with the wit of age.

That loony ancient quick-change act,
Each night appears in a new show,
With a new angle and disguise...
A little dangerous to know.

So pull the wool over your eyes,
There is no way to draw the blind,
And if you stare him in the face
You're bound to lose your peace of mind
Until he exits from the scene
As a grey pallor, dull and static,
Chases off the magic act,
Lulling the insomniac.

Slowly dawn ignites the sky
Before sun bursts in its glory,
And transforms the light display.
Night is over. End of story.

Some tune to another channel,
Some find floor shows more appealing,
But nightlife here is a panel
Of plain glass in Danny's ceiling.

In memory of Danny Steinberg

Next to Godliness

Sister Delours hangs up her laundry
Just outside the convent door.
Her good and gentle Caribbean face
Is concentrated as she pins
Each garment in its place,
And hums a hymn.

Sister Delours hangs up her sober petticoats,
Practical brassieres, durable nun's gear.
The stretched and restrained elastic
Of a plump ecclesiastic.

Then one by one, a chorus line
Of pastel underpants appear
Named for each day of the week.
Monday is lemon yellow, Tuesday: shocking pink,
(Who said, "Blessed are the meek"!)
Wednesday: blue, today is Thursday…missing in action;
Friday: green; Saturday: violet, Sunday must be home
and dry.

The task done, she smiles with satisfaction
As they dance with wild undisciplined abandon
Underneath the brilliant sky.
Cavorting, undulating, giving way
To the Trade Wind's choreography trouvée.

A goat bleats, and the ocean, postcard blue,
Creates a glittering background for the scene.
Humble dried in God's great launderette,
The billowing pin-ups frame the view.

Sister Delours places her basket underneath the stairs,
And goes to say her prayers,
Then climbs into her Jeep, winding through hills
To teach the housebound simple sewing skills
With loving care.
Returning home, her capable hands
Unpin the fluttering clothes,
And humming her hymn, she folds
The sun-blessed nunderwear.

Shaker Rap

They didn't go in for copulation,
Which did away with their population,
So pretty soon there were no takers
For that old time no sex sect, the Shakers.

But I think their religion needs revival
If we're planning on the earth's survival,
So spread the word, sing a Halleluiah...
The Shakers ways may seem peculiar,
But if you want to save our lands,
When you feel the urge, just shake, shake hands.

If you think of love, just say a prayer
For the water and for trees and air.
We can shake away to a new solution,
We can shake away the world's pollution.
We can shake away to save the whale,
So, shake 'til you break the Richter scale.
Gonna shake our way out of stress and strife,
Gonna shake our way to a simple life.

Shake a limb, sing a hymn for those God forsakers,
And convert the flirts to become good Shakers.
If you feel a big and strong attraction,
Just shake 'til you get satisfaction.
Shake, shake until you lose your breath,
It'll work much better than the rhythm method.
Shake away the evil, shake away for good,
Shake away for unplanned parenthood.
Keep awake and shake until they say
That they've abolished Mother's Day.
And don't stop shaking even when
The congregation shouts "Amen!"

A New Order

There is a serene lady
In the neighborhood,
Dressed in white robes, white bonnet,
White bag, umbrella.
Alone and circumspect.
A habit for all seasons,
Fastidiously home made.
It's possible that she belongs to a religious sect,
But if not, how sublime.
Denying fashion, hem lines,
Shoulder pads, fads,
Waistlines, wasted money, wasted time.

There but for the trace of God
Is an issue I could skirt.
If there's a Sisterhood of the Immaculate Agnostics,
I'm ready to convert.
Give away the closets jammed with has-beens,
Bargains, disasters. And have just
Two plain robes. One on, one off.
Simplicity.
What greater religion could there be?

Yes, give it all to the needy
Now that I've seen the light.
Mother Theresa of the fashion starved,
I'd distribute major labels to those too weak to fight.
And be cleansed in the process.
Just a minute…could there be a sainthood in it?
Never mind. I'll be reborn, Hallelujah!
No decisions about what to wear.
It's the answer to my prayer.

Next time I pass that gentle lady in the street,
Will we confirm the Sisterhood should our eyes meet?

Consuming Passion

*Praying Mantis (mantis religiosa): predatory insect,
the female of which devours the male after mating.*

The mantra of the Praying Mantis
Sounds tedious, as any chant is.
It prays, but with instinctive force,
The male lets nature take its course,
And finds too late, his mate's devices
Bring on a sudden post-life crisis.

If only he had been prognostic,
And changed sects to Mantis Agnostic.
If he'd been celibate or gay
But no, poor fool, in prayer he lay.
An insect's life without distinction,
Whose instincts led him to extinction.

And she, did she say grace, the sinner,
Before she ate her mate for dinner?

Nature is infinitely complex
Joining insects in sects in sex.

Sunbathing in Trieste, 1954

The women of Trieste,
Their blue veined monolithic thighs
And joyless sagging breasts,
Lay naked and refreshed themselves
In the sun by the sea,
In a sea of flesh.

And we, young and firm,
Disrobed modestly. Embarrassed
To walk among the mounds
Of overworked humanity.

We were free, unmarried,
And with the arrogance of youth,
You smiled and whispered,
"They weren't born,
They were quarried."

Those girls are strangers to us now,
And now, undressed,
No one would notice us
Among the ruins of the women of Trieste.

For Betsy Gehman

Ipso Fatso

I'm making a Will, the most willing of clients,
The money...let anyone grab.
More vital, I'm leaving to medical science
My major collection of Flab.

The pouches, the sacs and the bags are prepackaged,
They're waiting and ready to go.
My chins and my wattle, preserve in a bottle,
I've much more largesse to bestow.

In future, Professors will be the processors
Of all I'm most anxious to hide,
They can melt into candles or have my love handles
Transplanted on some skinny bride.

My bottom, they'll squeeze her into a deep freezer
'Til Reubens comes back into style,
Then some lucky model can wear my old waddle...
(The dimples come out when you smile.)

With hospitals willing, the idea is thrilling:
Establish the world's first Flab Banks,
Where any starved Mexican or anorexic can
Get plumped up free with my thanks.

Our cellulite layers may answer their prayers
As researchers labor and strive...
But I can't bear waiting...so think I'm donating
My blubber while I'm still alive.

Île Disposed

(Bea and Morris on the Île du Levant)

We have friends who go to France,
At small expense. Ex-pats sans pants,
Stay on an island in the nude,
And have a healthy attitude.

Nobody looks like Page Three copy,
Mostly they're overweight and floppy,
And do their washing in a basin
You wouldn't want to put your face in.

Nothing's luxurious or posh,
It's more Hieronymusly Bosch,
But they're devoted and unwilling
To admit it's damp and chilling,
And tiring holding in their gut
While strolling on the beaches. But
Next year same time they plan to spend a
Fortnight with the same agenda.

The Meter Reader

The doorbell rang.
A great heart-stopping noise.
There stood a little man in corduroys.
"I've come to read your meter" ...I could tell.
He flashed a little badge tucked under his lapel.
"The Poetry Society" it read.
And trembling I filled with fear and dread.
How much pentameter had I clocked up this quarter?
Could my quatrains sustain me and my daughter?

"We need to know what kind of verse you're doing,
Since your Poetic License needs renewing."

Descartes Before Diverse

I think, therefore
I am –
bic pentameter
I will discard
For something more
Spontaneous.

I think therefore
I'm too original
To rhyme.

Perhaps next time.

Incognito

She has taken to wearing the disguise
Of a middle-aged person.
Involuntarily.
Highly successfully.

She doesn't even recognize herself,
And is invisible to anyone
Outside the family who's under forty.

OD'd on vanishing cream,
They'd never dream
That underneath the wrinkles,
She can still think naughty.

Connoisseur

I love the ballet.
As I watch them plié
I keep wondering who's gay,
But by oath,
I could simply not say if
Dear Rudi Nureyev
Is AC or DC
Or both.

As he leaps through the air
With his taut derrière,
His thighs engineered
Like an ox.
His nostrils a-flare…
I think I know where
He conveniently keeps
His old socks.

Dressed to the Kilt

Where else but in a Scottish kilt
Can gentlemen, dressed to the hilt
And laden down in full regalia,
Still ventilate their genitalia?

The Winter They Took Away From Us

There is no They,
We do it to ourselves…
But how can we not?

So which came first,
The chicken or the pot?
We're the clucks who cook the chickens,
Who set the tables, who change the linens and chew the fat.
They love us. But do we need that?
Do we need it as a full time occupation,
When you should be painting for your life,
And I writing poems…
(This is a variation: a complaint),
But we ain't. Because what we need is a wife.

The Theys will gladly take it all,
Winters, Summers, off season breaks.
We're fully booked, overworked,
The most popular resort this side of the Atlantic.
And all free. Except for you and me,
Who pay with our vital juices.
In our guilt edged world,
Our houses are our nooses.

So paint the eggplants and the peppers,
Phooey to the ratatouille,
Let's behave like social lepers…
Serve them take-away chop suey!
And listen to your guru…keep repeating fast and slow,
The simple magic mantra that can change our lives,
It's "no, no, no, no, no…"

For Esther Rosen, 1984

Double Dactyls

Higgledy, Piggledy,
Hugo Von Hoffmansthal,
Wrote his libretti
With elegant style.
Tickled the tastes of
The intelligentsia.
If you're in MENSA, you'll
Roll in the aisle.

Nickity, Nackity,
Gloria Vanderbilt.
Poor little rich girl
Without any chums.
Now she's found happiness
Unostentatiously....
Millions are wearing her name
On their bums.

Lickity, Splickity,
Herbert Von Karijan,
Lightning conductor
With Sturm und mit Drang,
He has no doubts
Of his place in the firmament...
God's masquerading
As his Doppëlgang.

Peanuts Envy

I'm jealous of those people who
Can nibble peanuts…just a few,
Take one or two with great restraint,
Then stop…with will power of a saint.

For me, and all of Nature's gluts,
They're put on earth to drive us nuts.

Gran Knees

When I was a little sap,
I jumped onto my Grannie's lap,
And she cried out immediately:
"Oh, no, no...that's my bad knee!"

And so I thought old people had
One knee that's good and one that's bad.

Well now I'm an old granny too,
I think, How smart I was...they do!

Thank You, William Morris

For the willow boughs on my spread and pillow
That instantly transform
The chaos of an unmade bed,
With a laying on of hands,
Into an artful woodland, a bower of
Languid leaves and
Pre-Raphaelite sensibilities,
That sweep me to dreams
Of Utopia.

Bullocks View of Arvon Poets...Sheepwash, Devon

Look at them...a new flock of vegetarians
Phrasing on the grass.
I hear they're an endangered species,
Poets, so I'll let them pass.

They look harmless...almost picturesque,
A migratory lot. They'll soon be gone.
A restless breed these poets,
Swooping in, then mooo-ving on.

Oh, my Cud! That one's got red and white hooves-
A real aberration. Catch it quick before it moooves.

Just how important to the balance of nature
Are poets, anyway?

A moooot point, I dare say.

The Arvon Foundation gives five day residential courses in all disciplines of writing. They take place in amazing locations in Devon, Shropshire and Yorkshire, and are fascinating experiences in immersion with people you are never likely to meet in your personal orbit. Each group has two distinguished tutors and sixteen avid members. They all write, cook, dine, drink and quickly become deeply connected in the process.

I have taken three courses over the years, all at the magical Totleigh Barton in Sheepwash, Devon, and always choosing tutors with a light touch: Gavin Ewart, Wendy Cope, Roger McGough and Carol Ann Duffy, who is now England's first woman Poet Laureate, and a Dame. Then, she was a fresh and inspiring new voice building a reputation. Now, firmly established, her individual vision, strength and wit continue to amaze and delight.

Poetry Reading, London

I suffer fools gladly,
And by the plateful.
The one sure loser in a crowded room
Bores in on me,
And I am grateful.

Once I bought Wendy Cope a drink,
She took it and walked off to quaff
Among her galaxy, of course.
But I was not alone for long.
The Flotsam found its Jetsam
Like a magnetic force.

I hear myself drone every tired cliché,
No hackneyed phrase is spared.
On onomatopoeia-pilot, eyes glacé.
While all around the room vibrates
With real poets speaking in blank verse,
Inside jokes shared with knowing laughter.
While we, with our twin curse,
Are joined, no doubt, for ever after,
Two outcasts undisguised,
The fact belabored:
We're merely the Anthologized,
Anons among the chosen Fabered.

Fantasia on a Place Named Fressingfield

Remember our picnic at Fressingfield?
We took lunch in a box
A pick-up of snacks,
Ate lox on the rocks,
A nosh of a meal,
With paté and pickles,
Then lay on our backs
In the new mown hay's prickles,
And pulled off our socks.
While we were undressing,
Sipped vin ordinaire,
And while we were brushing
The straw from our hair
We never stopped fressing:
Brie, oozing on crusts
Of bread, cherries, strawberries
A Lucullan spread.
And since time wasn't pressing,
And we hadn't a care,
We lolled and we rolled
'Til our hunger was sated,
Sufficed in Suffolk,
Deliciously fêted,
All pleasures unpeeled
In Fressingfield.

Geographic note: Fressingfield is a village in Suffolk, England. Population over 900 (someone must have just had a baby). Two shops, three churches.

Linguistic note: Fressing is the Yiddish word for noshing.

County and Western

London's no place for a poet,
Rural's where word music thrives,
Near the setting suns of Dorset,
Where the rhythm is life giving…
Leave while there's still time to live in
Ryme Intrinseca.

Roll that round your tongue and palate,
What an address for a poet!
Or pack your Poetic License,
Try to put your life in order
Somewhere in a Summer setting
Scene across the subtle border.
Even if you're Muslim, Jewish,
Who could not help loving living
In Huish Episcopi?

What's in a name?
Only poetry.
With this geography at hand,
It must be Laureate Land.

Kissing the Blarney Stone

Given a tourist attraction or a three star restaurant,
We always drive right by,
Preferring serendipity and picnics off the road.
And so we wondered why so little architecture met the eye
As we drove through the Irish countryside.
Was it all Cromwell's fault?
The scenery didn't seem to care,
"Just take me as I am. There's time to spare."

The air was soft, the color, green,
That Spring day in the sixties
As we drew to a halt,
And climbed the gentle rise
Where Blarney Castle's ruins met our eyes.

Whatever it had meant in history
Was dimmed and far outshone
By the myth and mystery
Of the Blarney Stone.

Can you climb to the turret merely to observe the view?
Ignore the tempting act of trite indignity?
You can't pretend you're there for any other reason.
To flee the tower now would seem like treason.

But what am I doing in a place like this?
I'm lying on my back, trusting my life to
A dubious looking old leprechaun holding down
My legs, while I drop my head backwards
Over the precipice.
I see the world upside down for miles around,
Indelibly etched, each leaf, each patchwork meadow.
Aware of every shimmer, every sound.
Too startled by the beauty ,momentarily
I forget the kiss, forget that this
Is an ideal pose for a beheading,
Forget the fear that I'll slip into the abyss.

Then grasping the two rods, stretch to reach the stone
Some foot or two away and kiss the germs
Of thousands of other fools just like myself.
Small comfort that I'm not alone.

How will I know if I've received the gift of tongues,
The flow of gab, the loosening of images
The begetting of Begorrah?

Oh, they snap your photo and of course you buy it.
Who'd refuse? It's proof you've done the trick.
We laughed, it was a riot,
Then we tucked them away forever.
Instant memorabilia , tourist's treasure.
I don't remember ever seeing them again.
But then…

The snapshots lost, the memory blurred.
It's possible I have the stone to thank for every word.

Life, Death and Harpsichordian Dreams

To the extremes of Oxfordshire to hunt a harpsichord.
Not quite as esoteric as it sounds...
The piano can be heard through every floor,
Our building resonating to its core.

And as we drove, following maps,
The countryside unfolding toward our mission,
A tiny village with an old house-turned-to-shop
Appeared, just at the crossroads of my déjà vision.

Inside, wall to wall, elaborate gilded works of art,
Double keyboards, black on ivory,
Or the reverse. Spinets, clavichords, virginals. The thrill
Of fantastic Baroque imaginations.
Delicate Italian variations, French elegance, solid German,
Unadorned English examples of contemporary skill.

Their lids closed, side by side in rows,
They could be coffins, the elongated wooden cases.
But these weren't fashioned to be buried or be burned,
And there were no morticians with long faces.

A revelation! Suddenly I understood that here's the way
To play my life away,
Aspire to "Jesu, Joy of Man's Desiring,"
And my desire is no mere whim, but firm as rock,
A quid pro quo, since I will have no burial, not give in
To all that fol de rol and bumbling organs mutilating Bach.

With a well tempered casket now, instead,
Not dead wood, but resonant, vibrating life,
I can attempt to tame its high strung ways...
Enough to placate, but not wake the dead,
Or neighbours just upstairs, more to the point.
So back to Bach, Mozart, Scarlatti,
The sacred keyboard Trinity.
And if I play past midnight on a fling,
The people upstairs will not hear a thing.

Platform Performance

Wanted: Further information re: incident at Earl's
Court Station

As my train pulled into the station
I heard the reverberation of a barking dog.
High drama on the Westbound platform,
A travelogue in the heat of summer sun.
But I'd just missed Act One.

Center stage: Mr. Punch enraged.
Red hair, redder face, mouthing obscenities.
Is this a Comedy? Is this Eumenides?
No, it's a mime accompanied by barking dog.
(This train is Barking bound...
And my seat's on the aisle of dogs, sans dialogue.)

Wait...he's not Mr. Punch. Read his T-shirt.
It says "Captain Condom." With wildly jungular shorts
Designed for uninvented sports,
So loud they drown him out;
And on a short chain, a straining Rottweiler,
All teeth and snout, pulls him away from the crowd.

The Extras gather 'round the object of his fury.
Are they a Greek Chorus or a jury?
They observe a cowering Alsatian
Leashed to its master, a paunchy, balding gent
Whose light blue T-shirt...I promise you,
Reads: «Je Suis Enciente.»

This is the scene I scan,
When macho Birth Control patrol
Meets his first pregnant man.

And then my train pulled out, God wot,
I'd give a lot to know the plot
Did Mr. Punch cum Condom's Randy Rottweiler attempt
To rape «Je Suis Enciente's» Fräulein Alsatian,
That hot mid-summer afternoon in Earl's Court
Station...
Or not?

It's doggerel boggling stuff, this beat,
When man and beast are all in heat.

Eyebrowsing

I saw an old man passing by
As I walked out on Putney High,
So strange, though I'm not one to pry,
I had to look him in the eye.
The left one, which is all I saw,
Because his eyebrows, white as straw,
We're each obeying their own law...
A vision you could not ignore.

One swept up, lilting toward the sky,
All jaunty, if a bit awry,
A highbrow eyebrow to defy
The laws that gravity supply.
The other lowbrow, drooped forlorn
Below the lid, its orb to mourn,
A shaggy curtain to be shorn,
Unless...the eye beneath was gorn!!
What was it meant to signify...
A fashion statement...or a sty?

I'll never cease to wonder why
That odd man had, on Putney High,
One public and one private eye!

A Lady in Our Neighborhood

She walks erect with a deliberate stride,
Her body lithe, perhaps a dancer.
Always brightly clad in jeans or overalls,
A jaunty scarf around her head.

Yet, half way across Putney Bridge
You see the nest of hair looks
As if it had been dipped in black ink,
The cheeks are scarlet, painted with
An Impressionists careless hand.
The lips, a red smudge moving constantly.
The face of an old Toulouse-Lautrec harridan.

Like those split picture books where
You mix odd heads and bodies,
Hers don't match…the combination is absurd.

Always alone but in animated conversation,
Her eyes look inward.
Well past the age of a free bus pass,
She marches with vigorous aplomb,
Head held high, she leads her own parade.
Her inner life a vivid entity,
Invisible to you and me.

Jenny and Becky

We keep ourselves to ourselves,
Said the ancient sisters, proudly.

Frail and independent, refusing assistance,
They had simplified their lives
Into non-existence.

Artichoke Dream

The doorbell rang demandingly.

At the door was Maureen Shepherd, the General's wife
Who lives downstairs. There were two indistinct people
Hovering behind her.

"I've been telling them" said the General's wife,
The true commander in the family,
"What a good cook you are,
So we've come to see for ourselves."
"Come in," I said in full panic...
We had just enough to eat for our small party.
So Freddy gave them a drink, suspending our
Faceless friends in limbo.

I looked in the fridge, the pantry. Nothing.
So I slipped out and ran over the bridge to Putney.
Everything closed. On to Harrods. (this was a dream))
All closed.
Breathlessly came home hoping no one had noticed my
absence.
Looked in the pantry again.
There were only two tins of artichoke hearts,
And there was some watercress in the fridge.
I arranged them on three plates,
And announced to the General's wife:
"We're having a Zen supper tonight,"

Then awoke greatly relieved.

Moral: I have never since been without at least two tins of
hearts of artichokes in the larder. It's my Social Security.

*Note: Caravaggio was known to have split someone's face open
over a disagreement about artichokes. Certainly worthy of a battle,
but what was the disagreement about? How they should be eaten?
Does one use finger bowls or wipe the butter on your sleeve...oh,
why didn't I study Art History?*

Curriculum Vitae

I used to be a background singer…ooh,
That's what I used to do…be-do-be-doo.
A career that could clearly go far…wah-wah-wah,
Name an octave and I could do-aah…do-aah.

As a Katydid, Tattler, Dave and a Dame,
Or simply a group that ooh-aahed with no name,
I'd a knack for the track on the backside of fame,
And was gladly upstaged by the star…la-di-dah.

To enhance Perry, Ella or Lena or Frank,
We anonymous voices oozed out from the rank,
And if ever there's anyone I'd like to thank,
It's my teachers at Juilliard who moaned when I sank
To the depths, while I jingled my way to the bank.

Ta-daaah!

L'aprés Midi d'une Choeur

It's hell
To sing Ravel.

The lyrics are tricky
In *Daphnis and Chloe*.
Try making "Ahs" sexy,
And fermez "Mmmms" showy.

The counting, the waiting,
The sitting, the standing,
The re-takes, the tea breaks…
It's all so demanding.

But true to the spirit,
We're Impressionistic…
A bit vague on notes,
But extremely Artistic.

The je-ne-sais quoi
Of our texture is rich,
And comme il faux pas,
We're all nearly on pitch.

Our delicate line
Is as fine as a thin shell,
Authentically lilting
In pure French Previncial.

The esprit de chorus,
Is better than pay…

But next time I'll try
For the corps de ballet.

June 28, 1981, EMI, Abbey Road Studios
Daphnis and Chloe, Andre Previn, LSO, and Ladies of the
London Symphony Chorus

Musing

In my small way I tried to play the part
Of Patroness to Music's sacred art,
Aspiring to be the inspiration
Of the Nadia Boulanger generation.

I'd been adored by several young composers,
But the beds I cultivated were no beds of roses.*
At first I got a few atonal mentions,
Eclectic themes and immature pretensions,
But I was in a compromised position,
When none of them came up with a Commission.

And then I met a Tin Pan Alley cat,
Who showed me where the tunes were really at.

He set me to music.
Just a smooth ballad that a pop star got rich on.
The kind of thing a girl like me would never switch on.
I'd rather have inspired a work like Tristan and Isolde
To reminisce about when I grew older.
I'd sooner have been vocalized by Fischer-Dieskau
Than disco'd to in some saloon in San Francisco...

BUT, he set me to music,

A sentimental little arioso,
Crooned by a toupee'd aging Mafioso.
Oh, what did Alma Mahler have that I was lacking…
Could it have been the Viennese Arts Council's backing?
I'm immortalized by Muzak, not quite my dream come true,
You might even get to hear me in a public loo.
If I'm cynical, my pinnacle's amok,
Not top of the Poppea's…just plain poppycock…
BUT, he set me to music.

* Note: this is poetic license, I never bedded any of them.

Water Music

The pleasure boats slide by
Summer nights on the Thames,
Thrumming in the distance
So that you feel the pulse
Like a heartbeat before
You hear the music,
Making Charles Ives cacophonies
As they pass each other.
Silhouetted figures dance,
Gather on the decks,
Disco lights kaleidoscope
On the black water,
The water.

In the first light of dawn
A huge yellow helicopter
Hovers noisily at the River's edge
Slowly searching,
Whipping trees into a frenzied hurricane.
A black cat, arched in terror,
Is blown across the path.

It is no longer extraordinary

That even fish are terrified of water,

Or that we Pisces have

A fear of swimming.

Aqua poorer, the element we cannot live without,

And cannot live within;

That swallows the innocent, the beautiful,

And then continues on

As if they'd never been.

*In memory of Chris Garnham and the victims of the Marchioness
disaster, August 20, 1989.*

My Brother, Dying

Ironic that the one with all the brains
Lies propped up on the pillows, eyes closed,
Tawny beard and vulnerable mouth,
His head half shaved. The curved incision
Stapled together crudely
As an awkward parcel.
Startling, considering what it holds.
Today his eyes don't open,
But his head moves restlessly.
I talk to him, play Mozart, read aloud,
Gently rub his neck and his right arm,
The one with feeling, in the few places
Left exposed where tubes and tape permit,

The hours pass, the intravenous drips.
I hold his hand. The scientist,
Mathematician, chess champ, violinist…
No more. All down the drain.
The brain drain.
"The good die young," my Mother says,
"He worked his brain too hard."
And they say there's a God.

In memory of Richard Cook Gilbert, 1925-1987

68

Exits

For practical advice don't turn to poets,
They never get it right.
Go gently and as peacefully as possible
Into that Good Night.

And if you think you've made a big impression,
Forget that last encore.
Just bear in mind the old expression:
"Always leave 'em wanting more."

To My Grandson on His First Day on Earth

This is the first day of the rest of your life,
To coin a phrase.
And since you have no past,
The opportunities are vast.

Mine starts here too.
I have a whole new life with you.

Optimism

Now that I'm sixty, I concede,
I'll never dance in Les Sylphides.
I won't get greener in the eyes,
Nor likely, win the Nobel prize.
No chance that I'll reach five-foot-four,
Or learn to love to scrub a floor.
Too late to be a wunderkind
Or make up for my sins unsinned.
I'm willing to acknowledge that
I may not lose my baby fat.

Yet I'm convinced…that come what may,
I'll be discovered any day.

PART TWO

OUTWITTING GRAVITY

Poems 1995 – 2015

Outwitting Gravity...Ode to 83

Still winging it.

Some day I may land in a place
I mean to stay.

Meanwhile, I occupy this space
It seems.
Were I to flap my wings and fly away,
To satisfy my dreams,
I'd have to lose a stone,
(That's fourteen pounds),
To lift me off the ground.
And I like lunch too much,
So I'm earth bound.

Fact is, I like it here,
And so, although I mutter,
I think I'll leave it to the birds to flutter,
And tuck my wings away,
For all their charms...
(Besides, the damn elastic hurts my arms.)

So, like the Emu, this old bird
Will sit it out...with one last word.
The flight of fantasy
Is oxygen to me...
It's my last laugh,
Outwitting gravity.

Merci M. Montaigne

There are five advantages to old age
According to Monsieur Montaigne,
And he was a Frenchman, remarkably sage,
The wisest man in la campagne.

So here, for filling up your mental tank,
Are the cinq:

Une: One's memory is bad…or mal,
(There's God knows who to thank)

Deux: One can't be a good liar.
(Though you may be a great crank).

Trois: One cannot tell long stories.
(Since your mind may well go blank).

Quatre: One forgets offences.
(Since you've lost your memory bank).

And I can't remember cinq.

Heavenly Parties...November 21st, The Times

God threw a little birthday bash for Voltaire and Magritte,
The only way the two of them were ever bound to meet.
Magritte discreetly doffed his bowler hat at Voltaire's bust
Upon its lofty pedestal, and brushed aside the dust.
He poured a glass of bubbly, and then clearing his esophagus,
Inquired, "How did you manage to escape from your
sarcophagus?"
Voltaire gave him a thoughtful stare and raised an eyebrow
quizzically,
"Monsieur, you can be sure it was maneuvered metaphysically."

Then Arthur Quiller-Couch appeared, his beard and wings
askew,
"I say, old chaps, the slightest lapse...my birthday, too!" said Q.
A murmur of embarrassment enveloped the Sublimes,
"Well, how was I to tell," said God. "It wasn't in The Times."

Schopenhauer's Mask

*"The closing years of life are like the end of a masquerade party,
  when the masks are dropped."*
  ~ *Arthur Schopenhauer, philosopher, 1788-1860 (age 72)*

As Schopenhauer said,

Before you're dead,

The masks are dropped.

There's no need to pretend

That things are other than they are

When life is drawing to its end.

How true, but the cruel fact

Is that in later life,

Before quite giving up the ghost,

The mirror shows, although you're still in tact,

You need the mask the most.

But how would a philosopher who,

Though he's deemed a sage,

Merely in his seventies presume to gauge

The real meaning

Old Age?

No Cause For Alarm

If you start waking up very early,
When you get to be seventy-five,
It's because you can't wait to discover
Whether you' re dead or alive.

Then you open The Times with your coffee,
See what the Obits have to say,
And if you find that you're not listed,
You're ready to start a new day.

Sole Searching

By God, I have been shod.
I cannot count the ways.
My leather bound pediography
Name drops like an operatic libretto.
A farrago of Ferragamos, Amalfis,
Capezios have danced through my life…

I never reached Imelda's heights
Stilettos…stilts on toes,
The archenemy of womankind,
While I have splurged on wedgies,
And nearly subterranean pancake heels…
Sensuous sandals on the Lido in Venice.
And properly footed for Hurlingham tennis.

No Manolo Blahnik, who caused panic on the pavement,
Enslavement to high fashion…at least three inches higher
Than the rest, while chic freaks all walk en pointe,
repressed.
His name will never cross my instep.
For cheap thrills,
Let's talk espadrilles.

And as for Jimmy Choo and Christian Laboutin,
Their astronomic fame and prices,
So refined, but can they say
That humans were designed
To walk that way.
What good Christian would choose to torture women so?
(And jimmy up their prices as they go)
A Theologic crime perhaps? I'd like to know.

I think, for what it's worth,
They'd better hurry back to earth,
Before they land there on their faces
Head over heel, with the turn of
Time and Fortune's wheel.

Watch these spaces.

Fashion Statement

This year, I hear that crêpe is in.
For once I'm really chic.
I'm swathed in it…observe my skin,
The neck, the arms, the cheek.

And pleats are all the rage, says Vogue…
At last, I'm really hip
In rivaling Fortuny…
Just above the lip.

Veiled Confession

I would like equal rites.

I'd want them lightweight,
White, drip dry and well cut,

Wouldn't I love to be on
The inside looking out.

No one to judge me by my face,
My age, my hair, my skin,

Only my eyes and my voice.

I know I'm not alone,
And although I want to Liberate
The Women of the World
As much as the next Enlightened female,
Why don't we try changing places first.

We may envy them their privacy.
And understand why they don't all
Want to drop the veil.

Go and Catch

Go and catch a falling arch,
Set sail on a root canal,
Hear a drummer, join the March,
Swim across the Mer de Mal,

Play a String Theory quartet,
Have a thought and catch its train,
Mingle with the croquet set,
Wax, perhaps, but never wane,

Scoff at fools who still write rhyme,
Whistle through a mermaid's tooth,
On this journey, veiled in time,
Show me where I lost my youth.

If it isn't to be found,
Never mind, I'll hang around.

Mr. Mackovicka's Wings, Prague, 1972

From a Photo by Miroslav Hucek

He is standing on a little square table
Near the edge of a roof.
Neighboring houses spread below,
A cathedral in the distance.

Tense in the moment of truth,
Harnessed with strings,
His arms spread out against the sky,
Attached to wings he has no doubt
Spent years amending.
Gossamer paddles
Whose feathery ends intend to fly.

Geared for ascending,
A solemn man, cloth cap
And horn rimmed glasses, sturdy,
His knees are slightly bent, ready...
But first:
LOOK AT THE BIRDIE!!!

What happened, Mr. Mackovicka aka Icarus,
After Mr. Hucek clicked his Leica?
Did you soar over Prague's rooftops,
Or fall from the sky?

I need to know
Before I try.

Boundless

My wings itch.
Actually, it itches
In the place my wings should be:
Neurotic zones
That make vestigial remnant instincts
Stir my bones…in places
I can't reach.

Their time has come.
Walking is hell on heels. I dread
The leaden pavement's thrum.
My soles have lost their will to tread,
And shoes should be ashamed.
There's no excuse
Confining us, hide-bound
To their abuse, when we were born
To be footloose.

I know a gentle waft
Could send me, self propelled, aloft,
As simply as birds fly,
As easily as breathing,
I could catch a tailwind by its tail
And sail the sky.

Old Age Is . . . . .

You don't want to know.
But I'll tell you anyway.
It's for the birds.
Old feather dusters,
All tweets and clusters
Taking wing,
Flying and dying in one final fling.

And it's from hunger.
Lost its appetite,
Its zing and its zest
For feats and fests,
The herbs and rare spices
That ring in the seasons,
That give life desire
Gone out with the fire,
Have lost all their reasons.

For the Brave?
Nothing heroic
To be one left standing.
Just to survive
And staying alive.
The mere lack of dying
Means you can't be trying.

Treadmill to Oblivion

The Dalai Lama takes his exercise. (New Yorker photo)

Here is a Guru for our times,
One we can trust,
No prayer wheels or wind chimes,
No lotus pose or standing on his head
Gathering dust.
Instead, he plods the real world,
Walking to Infinity
Just like the rest of us.

His is the path to tread
One step at a time.
A never-ending thread,
No valleys and no peaks to climb.
No traffic or road rage.
It's, as they say who know,
Simply a time to disengage.
The way to go.

Rejoice, and why go anywhere?
It's possible there may not be a There.

Returning

First of all, the water and the sky.

I have been thirsty for this view,
Confined to walls and looking out
At other peoples windows,
Into other people's lives.
My own is quite enough

Here my vision stretches to infinity
And no one's looking back at me.
Beyond the yachts and obscene luxury,
Above, beyond the sea,
(Today an idyll of tranquility),
Is the vast sky,
A moving picture show
Never the same twice.
Then the horizon
You can't get bored with this for scenery.

Just looking, thanks. No need to buy
What's free to every eye.

Is there a better place?
Not for the likes of me.
Although there used to be,
But here, I rest my case.

Returning to Florida, November 2014

Florida, the Seasons

Winter is, or so I'm told,
Always unseasonably cold.

Spring, a harbinger of what?
This year's unseasonably hot.

Summer, Weather Man explains,
Will bring a string of hurricanes.

And Autumn, which I used to love,
Contains most of the above.

With Florida for inspiration
Vivaldi'd have no reputation.

Condo Christmas

'Tis the season to be merry,
So make certain that the wreath'll
Not drip poison from the berry,
Mind! The holly's scratch is lethal.

And the tree, that joyful symbol,
What a sight it is, begorrah,
Here good will could fill a thimble.
Fight it out, crèche and menorah!

Fa-la-la, the Wise Guys' journey,
Fallen angels in full voice
Hire themselves a smart attorney.
Let us join hands and rejoice!

Peace on Earth, good will to men…
Can anybody tell us when?

The Three Questions...
(well, maybe four, but who's counting?)

If Jesus was Jewish...
Then tell me this:
Who was invited to the Briss?

And his Bar Mitzvah,
IF and WHEN...
No relics?
No gold fountain pen?

And furthermore,
Just to annoy...
What kind of a name is Jesus
For a nice Jewish boy?

The Trouble With Florida

The trouble with Florida is as follows:

You reach a Golden Age
And move to a Golden climate,
Surrounded by sunlight
And mirrored walls that don't leave you alone.

Their dazzling reflections reveal
An old hag you almost recognize
And don't much like the look of.
She won't go away...
This doppelganger is
Ganging up on you.
You try to ignore her
But she keeps catching your eye.
You can't escape.
Every wrinkle, bulge, sag
Follows you in a pas de deux
Of identical twins.

Forget about a Bad Hair Day...
Every day in Florida is a Bad Face Day,
A Terrible Body Day.

There's a lot to be said for taking the Veil.
I might convert.

Incident on the Ides of March 2007

She who stole my purse is trash,
But she, who also filched from me
My good name for the cash,
Stole my identity, which robbed me two-fold.
And her game? Attack by knife-point,
Flee, skid out of sight.

The wound's more than skin deep
As I replay the scene night after night.

What's in a name? A knack for forgery,
But not my life.
Within my purse there lay
A chance more valuable than vice
If she'd played my cards right.
The libraries, museums,
Classes at the University.
Her future, if she'd lived my true identity
Might just have shown her there's another way.

But then, she is a slave, addicted.
And now she's caught, I'm me again
In my own name, and she's convicted...
Though having crossed her path,
I too, will never be the same.

P.S. A car! A car! my condo for my car!
She grabbed the keys and nabbed my Grand Marquis...
Which shouldn't come as a surprise to me,
Since Mercury's the God of Thievery!!

Legs

Climbing the steep staircase
To the entrance of Good Samaritan
For my annual mammogram,
I followed a pair of legs
Several steps above me.
Wearing white shorts…(this is laid back Florida),
They were smooth, tanned, unblemished,
And perfectly formed, from gently
shaped calves, to elegant ankles
Tapering into the ubiquitous tennis shoes.

Those legs, I thought,
Have never borne babies,
Stood hours at a sink or ironing board.
Those legs have never cooked a meal
In their life.
They are a gift,
Like a beautiful singing voice
Or the ability to paint, or red hair.

We reached the top in sequence.
The glass doors slid open,
And the legs turned to the left
As I walked straight ahead.

Looking back, I caught a glimpse of their owner…
A middle aged man with a paunch and gray hair.
He carried a big bouquet of flowers,
No doubt for his wife.

I hoped she wasn't dying of envy.

Bird Song From a Parked Car

Five strands of telephone wire
Strung out against a dove grey sky.
A flock of birds swoop down
And perch haphazardly.

They look to me like Mocking Birds,
Who lurk in all the trees I park beneath
Their message is their medium,
And yet, I always opt
For shade, and take what's dropped.

Ach, Nein! These are not Nachtigals!
It's daylight, and we have no call for Liede here.
This is a neighborhood where
Boom boxes assault the air and ear.

But birds don't care about their names or breed,
Or how they breathe…they can't sight read.
They simply open up their throats
And sing the notes.
I watch them pause from flight,
While traffic separates me from their calls.
They take their places,
And I see they're staved in thirds,
Each one a plump black note that fills the spaces.
Against the pale sky.
An avian manuscript.

Well, I can SING these birds!
So, I'll try trilling…
Unseen, I join their high wire act.
It's thrilling!

Then suddenly they fly away,
And I am sitting waiting in a Buick
Outside Walgreens,
On Route One, FL, USA.

The flock has lots to sing about,
It's Spring, they're heading North,
And they can meet to practice in their choirs
Wherever there are high line wires.
But I am left with one regret:
Their music is ephemeral, and now they're gone.
I haven't got the hang of it just yet,
But have a hunch I could perfect their song.

You think they'd notice if I revved the car and tailed along?

Web Sights

August mornings, the hot sun
On the East facing window brings
New marvels every day.

Spider webs;
Ingeniously intricate inventions,
Constantly improvising their theme with variations,
What ever comes their way...
A dead fly, a dried leaf, a tiny moth still winging it,
All spun, impromptu
Into a gossamer roundelay
Embellished with dew drops,
Sparkling like misplaced gems.

I'm a purist,
And I prefer to see the miracle
Of their basic geometry unimproved.
Watch as they recreate
The pattern in their DNA
Compelling them to
Weave their lives away.
It seems a sacrilege, but I too
Start to feel entrapped
Inside Nature's net curtains,
So I gently ply a feather duster,
Like some cartoon orange bird,
To disconnect the works of art.
They collapse reluctantly,
A few strands clinging hopelessly
To the window's edge.

Caught in the act,
Their maker scurries quickly in retreat,
Hiding off stage until the time is right.
We both wait expectantly.
And it begins again,
Woofing and warping in the air,
An embroidery it cannot stop.

Something resonates.
Weaving our lives over and over
In repeated patterns.
Spinning the weeks
Threading the months,
Looming the years
Until they're swept away
Like cobwebs
On an August day.

Momento Mori

Uncle Lou died this morning,
And they brought his remains to my kitchen:
A half eaten box of Cheese Snax, one small jar
Of strawberry jam, a jar of instant coffee,
Pumpkin bread, a yellow apple, a packet of Swiss cheese,
And an opened box of Uneeda biscuits.

While they made the funeral arrangements,
I tried to find a place for the legacy.
In jockeying the Uneeda biscuits into line,
I knocked over a large unopened jar of Dijon mustard.
It cracked open, gushing over the tins of food
Onto the white tile floor,
Filling the morning air with an inappropriately
Pungent smell.

I picked up the guilty carton and looked inside.
There were two crackers left…
And we don't even like Uneeda Biscuits.

On my knees, wiping up the mess and broken glass,
A phrase came from the past
And wouldn't go away
"Too old to cut the mustard."

Lou would have loved that, I thought.
At heart he was a song and dance man
The mantra repeating in my head.
This is a fitting way, since I can't pray,
To wipe away the shock and sadness.
It's the least I can do,
A syncopated fair thee well to Uncle Lou.

Faces in the Audience

There's T. S. Eliot on the aisle.
Perhaps he's visiting Palm Beach
To lighten up his somber style
Or find those mermaids singing each to each.

Now, Carole Lombard sweeps into our row,
All smiles and gilded in lamé,
With…look! It's Frank Lloyd Wright in tow,
I'd know him anywhere, the old roué!

Recycled from the grave? A masquerade?
Surely these relics live no more.
Or is it that old people as they fade,
All look alike, or like someone you've seen before.

Tulip Diary, May 4, 2014

The purple tulips that you brought,
And I put carelessly in a low glass bowl
In the center of the table,
Have opened this morning,
And are continuing last night's lively conversations.

There's one facing me at breakfast, agape.
Its white tongue and black stamen
Surrounded by flared mauve petals
Has an urgency in its confrontation…
Is there something I forgot to say?

The others are more self-contained,
But each faces one of last night's guests
As if they were still around the table,
Listening to the animated talk. All ears.

I loved that we were many ages,
And different backgrounds,
And the joy of discovery
That poured out,
And yes, the love.
To say nothing of the
Delicious contributions..
Oh, Ozgur's marinated lamb!!

Those tulips facing East,
Elissa's laughter fed them oxygen.
And David's resonating bass
Turned wisdom to delight.
Indelible, this night.
Alex took it in,
Claudia exulted on a theme.
Esra, smiling quietly in anticipation,
Ozgur's expansive ease
Fred poured and had a story,
And I…will never be without
A conversation of tulips again.
They are the after-life of the party.

Monday:

The purple tulips are reaching out
In every direction, wide open
And expectant,

Where has everyone gone?
We need to talk.

Tuesday morning:

They're letting it all a hang out.
A Disappointment of tulips
Facing each empty chair,
Making me feel guilty
That we've abandoned them.
They're starting to droop.

Wednesday:

They refuse to give up.
Fading, swooping downward,
Pale and luminous,
Open winged, pleading.
The two of us
Ignoring them.
No sparkling repartee,
It's hardly worth their while.
Beginning to tinge at the edges,
But I can't throw them away until
They drop their petals.

Of course, they were always in their After Life,
The French are realistic,
What we call a Still Life,
To them is "nature morte."
Exactly.

Created to give momentary pleasure,
Waiting to die. No crime, it's just
Amazing that they had such zest,
Considering that they
Were cut off in their prime.

Thursday:

Instead of dropping their petals,
The tulips have remained in a state
Of perpetual immotion.
I promise not to anthropomorphize
Or put ideas into their heads,
But look at this: Two of them are not open
And floppy, but have returned to their original,
If faded form. They are closed, and one is
Pointing at the place where Esra sat. Beautiful,
Young, and very soon to become a Mother.
Is it waiting to open with her?
Ridiculous of course, like reading
Tea leaves. I must stop.

Still no dropped petals, so they must stay,
A strange centerpiece, indeed.
The leaves are starting to yellow.
We have guests coming tonight
For several days,
But they are Clinical psychologists,
So will understand completely.

I'll treat us to a new bunch tomorrow.
Our cleaner, with her romantic Cuban heart,
Came in and immediately cried:
"Oh, what beautiful flowers!"
"But they're dead, Ada."
She can see their strange enchantment.

They are casting a spell.
Perhaps by tomorrow they will simply be
Dead tulips. Ready to go.
I hope so.

It just occurred to me:
Why on earth didn't I take pictures?
But then, I wouldn't have been compelled
to write about them.
Did anybody notice?
There are ten of them,
One for each guest and two spares
Just to keep the action going.

Friday morning:

They have given up,
Lost the will to be center stage,
Dropped petals, turned ugly.
I have done the kind thing,
It is five a.m. and I take the bowl into the kitchen
And gather them into the rubbish bin.

I don't expect to have a relationship.
With my next bunch of tulips,

But their replacement will be chosen today.
Possibly tomorrow
Probably not purple.

Meanwhile, I replace my beloved green glass bowl,
On the table, filled with tempting
Apples, oranges, mangos, grapes.
How can this be nature morte when they are
There to feed us life.

And tulips?
Their lives were hardly still,
And yet their nature was always morte.

But they didn't pass unnoticed.

For Claudia Fry

Beaching

Untrustworthy, the sea.
I can't stand sand
Insinuating into every crevice of anatomy.

Bored to the teeth
With surf, and god forbid,
The stuff that's underneath.
What you can't see
Defies description,
Can bite or sting…or direly,
Might eat you up entirely.

So I'm entitled to my fears,
Here on Singer Island…
Where incidentally,
No one's heard a mermaid sing
For years.

Although, it's true that walking on the edge,
Firm sand pumicing your feet,
Searching for tumbled sea glass,
(Most prized are blue…
From old Milk of Magnesia bottles,)
As gentle water wavers in and out.
Is one of life's best things to do.

But as for the whole sea,
The great Atlantic,
It's too gigantic
For the likes of me.
Decidedly,
It's not my cup of tea.

A Lamentation On Swans

Is this to be my last Swan Upping
On the Thames?

One is aware, now time has past,
These swans were once for supping.
But now they're counted and protected
By the Queen
As carefully as her crown gems,
Each noted or ringed to date them.

Those Royal feasts are now long gone,
And swans are not as obsolete
As those who ate them.

The flock…or Sounding.
(Even if they're Mute)
Are bred no more for serving,
But for conserving,
Have no fear.

So, cast your bread upon the waters
They will return next year.
The Queen can count on that.

But I have no idea
If I'll be here.

Insomniata...2011

I cannot sleep.
My costly mattress
Doesn't do the trick.
(Does mattress ticking tick?)

A bed of roses?
Probably they'd prick.
A waterbed would seep,
And feathers make me sneeze...

Clouds!! That would be the answer.
I'm not hard to please.

Look! There's one now, it's wafting in the sky.
Is that Cloud Nine I've heard so much about?
I'll try to catch it when it passes by.
And then I'll nestle in its fleece.
Ah, Peace!

There is a possibility,
Sheep will be counting me.

Will wonders never cease!

Water Ways

It's not the drinking water I'll miss,
The hard stuff from our 1929 lead pipes
Supplied by Thames Water.

It's the Thames itself,
Ebbing and flowing outside my window
For the past forty years.

Magical hydrotherapy,
As I have watched its comings and goings
From my kitchen window seat.
Looking over the rose garden,
Beyond the swath of lawn,
The York paving stone path, the Hawthorne hedge,
The roof of the little rustic hut,
To the River.

A modest boat or two
Anchored within view.
Swans idling elegantly,
Ducks dipping or letting the tide
Lazily carry them with the flow.

A tourist boat may pass,
More frequently in Spring or Summer,
Or a party boat on Saturday nights
Thrumming with music.
And I keep an eye out for the Thames Bubbler,
An impressive blue and white affair,
Moving along at a purposeful clip
As it oxygenates the River so that
The first salmon in a century
Has been caught upstream.

I see over the wall of our Secret Garden,
The espalier fig tree has thrived too well,
And its leaves now block some of my view
Across the River to the park,
Sunday cricket matches on the lawn,
Families at play, a pair of police stroll on horseback.
And I watch the changing light, sunsets,
Reflections on the water,
No two the same.

Then there's my bathtub, as old as I am
Original when Rivermead Court was built,
Deep and long and the water comes
Hot and furiously fast.
A few drops of rose geranium oil
In the steaming water, ease slowly in,
And stretch out full length, free floating,
My head cradled in the now obsolete bath pillow.
Which of us will go first?
The tensions vanish.
I am nowhere.

Showers are for the New World,
With our dynamic view
Of the busy waterway,
The super yachts that
Bring out my socialist instincts
As I look the other way at
Black children playing in the park.

This view was a perfect contrast
As long as I knew I had the other
Quiet life to balance it.
Privileged for so long.
So long…
Now I must make peace
Within myself.
Goodbye, London,
The Snow Bird has landed.

Mistress of My Own Mattress

I have a Queen-size bed
And I am Queen of my domain!
My counterpane, a sea glass tint
That hints of an expansive view.
Oh, but I am a lucky Royal...
It makes my blood damn near turn blue.

This mattress, bought at Bloomingdales
In one of its prestigious sales.
The famous maker I've forgotten,
But do recall it's well named line:
"The Vanderbilt"...that made me smile.
Was it Trieste? No, no...Mannheim.
I see the bright white puffed duvet,
The Vanderbilt chasing me 'round the bed.
Catching my breath, I firmly said,
"Let's make this clear,
I am the Duenna, here to keep the peace
Between you two, my dearest friend and you.
It seemed like such a good idea...now this!
You see, As far as I'm concerned,
There's no Plan B."

At last he knew I meant it,
And consented to be friends instead.

Now he's long gone and I am old
Sinking into a dreamless sleep
With no regrets that
I was never the Vanderbilt mistress.
And yet, how sweet the irony, me deeply
Embedded in the Vanderbilt mattress.

A charming bloke…
I know he'd see the joke.

Viewpoint

The buzzing of a saw gets my Pavlovian juices flowing,
Cuts to the quick…it means another tree is going.
And yet I have revised those fixed emotions… and am not
torn,
This tree is dead, and I'm not here to mourn.

A tinge of schadenfreude, and yet, it's true
My faith in Fate's restored, and soon my view.
Now…there's the buzz! Run to the window for the show!
The Surgeon, helmeted, earmuffs, no gloves.
His face protected though, with goggles.
A safety belt around his waist. With ease
He wields his treacherous sword, and moves
As graceful as a leopard in the trees

He's lopped the upper branch and tossed it down,
Moves on to finish off its rusty crown,
At every level carving off a step, and each
Assures a foothold he can reach.

Sawing his way down, limbs fall to the ground,
Two helpers stack. He takes a respite from the sound,
Then back to re-attack. The droning calms
And soon all that is left are trunk and arms.
Then suddenly, it's terra firma, and the tree
Becomes an instant memory.

I can't believe the view! I'm stunned, I drink it in.
Hidden until this moment, yet where it's always been,
The River, nearly blinding in the sun
Moving as swiftly as my dreams were spun…
Piscean instincts swimming free,
A mesmerizing aqua therapy.

I fling the window open and applaud
The virtuoso, due his just reward.
He turns, looks up surprised, and then bows low,
An audience of one, a one-man show.

The tree is gone. In all these years, the shame
Is that I've never even known its proper name.

October 2009
I found out that it was a Red Maple…always dingy, it never
burst into glorious Autumn colors like the American version.
It probably never wanted to be there.

Three Ladies of Rivermead Court
(and one Gentleman)

Just as I'm leaving
I'm losing my ladies,
My precious old ladies
Inspired my life.
Joan died last night,
And I fear for the others.
Ann is in Hospital,
Mary's not right.

It's my shortbread circuit,
(I make it with ginger)
They said they're addicted,
And loved every bite.
Now Joan's gone forever,
It's sadly predicted
For both of the others
The end is in sight.

And then there's Sir John,
Who we've known for ages,
He can't walk or read
But his mind is still clear.
And we're both devoted
To John Betjeman's poems.
I read to him, but
Will he be here next year?

John's teaching me English,
As it should be spoken
(He's Eton and Cambridge,
And mine's a mere token.)
With poems and shortbread,
A good cup of tea,
The world's not as grim
As it was before 3:00.

Yes, life as we've known it at Rivermead Court,
For these forty years is a thing of the past,
Ephemeral joys, but alas, c'est la morte,
Like everything else, it was not made to last.

Joan, Lady Carnwath — d. September 2014
Mary Dickson Scott — d. November 2014
Ann Kemp-Gee — d. March 2015
Sir John Lambert — d. July 2015

Song Cycle: Homage to Fromage

á la Debussy:

The Camembert, the Brie,
That oozes, sets the Muses free,
Ah, oui, après midi,
C'est fromage.

After Britten: (with boy's chorus)

Stilton, creamy, crumbling,
Cheddar, strong, mature,
Cheshire, Caerphilly,
Humbling as we take our tasty tour,
Of the Suffolk shore
Of Britain.

After Rossini:

Bel Paese, Mozarella,
Provolone, Pastorella,
Parmesan I like a lotta
Grated, melted with Ricotta,
But my heart goes palpitate
With a perfect Dolcelatte.

Hymn:

Sing a hymn of praise and thanks
To Switzerland, for clocks and banks,
For chocolate and pure mountain air,
And finely knitted underwear,
For yodeling, but most of all:
Holy, Holy Emmental.

Strauss…Johann or Richard:

Nein, no Munster on my platter,
So meek and mild it does not matter.
But I'm crazy as a Nazi,
For Kummelkase, Schimmelkase,
Doplrahmfrischkase und Frustuck.
A whiff of Limburger, a winsome look,
And at last I found romance.
The zest, the zeitgeist,
Ach! The pong drove me to song.
You came along, and I found
Liederkranz!!

Mother Nature vs. God

Canto I

Who gets the blame
For natural disasters?
She does, of course.
Female hysteria, temper ablaze.
While He, with all his force,
Moves in mysterious ways.
His game
Is much more macho stuff,
Like wars
Fought in His name.

Canto II

Is Mother Nature Mrs. God, or what?
They don't seem to stay home alone a lot.
She's frantic with her earthly chores,
While he runs off and stirs up wars.

Chances are slim
That She believes in Him.

Extra Virgin

I've been looking at my olive oil bottle,
And my imagination's opened up full throttle.

Question: Who are these Extra Virgins?
Are there so many there's a surplus, an excess?
Or are some extra pure?
I'm not quite sure who changed the plot,
I thought you either were a virgin or were not.
And that they were as scarce as hen's teeth
Since the Pill. Perhaps abstention is the latest thrill.

What does it take to make an Extra Virgin?
Is she so chaste she's never had an urge?
Are the Italian hills all filled with cloisters
So crammed with Extra Virgins they can splurge?

And these Devouts, their prayers are seldom answered,
Although they have no sins for their confession,
Their chastity is finally rewarded
With a chilly thrill of what's called "Cold Compression."

If that's the lot of all the Extra Virgins,
What happens to the others, not so blessed?
Are they so unrefined that when they're tested,
Flunk out because they just loved being pressed?

Back to the olive groves they go those Virgins ordinaire,
If I were still a virgin I'd be glad to join them there.
Just lazing in the sun, a glass of wine and no regret
That they didn't make the grade for vinaigrette.

A Muse Remembers the Floating World

I'm in love with an older man...
Two hundred years older than I am,
And Japanese. He's Katagawa Utamaro.
I'd run away to him tomorrow if I could.

To see as he sees
A screen's transparency,
Voluptuous folds of fabric,
The elegance of line, defined in wood
That brings his floating world to life.

For that I'd gladly be his wife,
Lover, concubine...or if I could choose,
His Muse.

And while he's drying out his brushes
I'd prepare a plate of sushi,
Then we'd sip a cup of sake,
And while I massage his back he...
Ah, yes, I digress.

The hand that has caressed my breasts
Transposes all that tenderness
For other eyes to see.
My love is not a Samurai,
His pen is mightier than the sword.
Still mightier even than his pen...
He thrusts again, again.

In strokes that need no scholar to translate,
He then creates something sublime:
Art that outwits Time.

But could it be that Edo's not my Eden?
Life may be less delicious
If he's out sketching Geishas
While I'm home in a kimono
Washing dishes and noodling Haiku.
Might I regret my time warp wishes had come true?

A man can be ephemeral
As the breeze made by a passing fan.
So is it wise to think that
Truth lies filtered through his eyes?

It may well be, for all its grace and flowers,
His world was not a better one than ours,
And only time can distill art
Until it floats above reality.

Perhaps most geniuses
Are best left to posterity.

But, oh, the dream was ecstasy!

October 2013
Shunga Exhibition, British Museum

Disorientated

I have terrible Feng Shui,
All arranged the wrong way,
Not gung-ho for Kung Fu
And Tai Chi's not for me.
I've a deep fear that Sushi
Will broaden my tushi,
And I'm over-syllabic for classic Haiku.
(You might know that what ever I do
My kimono sleeves constantly
Fall in the Pho.)

Is it all overrated...
Am I on the wrong queue?
Or am I just ill fated....
Disorientated, decidedly dated
As Anna May Wong
And poor old Fu Manchu.

The Acronym That Dares to Speak Its Name
. . . Again & Again & Again

Acronyms save a lot of time,
And a film may lose its power
If they said, "For Unlawful Carnal Knowledge"
Instead,
We'd be there another hour.

After seeing "Birdman," February 2015

Do Not Forget
On Billy Collins' "Some Final Words"

We have the past to thank for
Everything we have become.
Since Now will soon be eaten up by Time,
Just think about amnesia, with no yesterday,
A vanishing tomorrow, and the moment on its way.

But then, you're not quite old enough to know...
Ago is like a luxury resort
Where you indulge yourself,
Replay, hold court,
Omit what's best forgotten on command...
And since the future doesn't look so hot,
In Once Upon a Time, you lead the band.

I hear the music, too,
It's Mahler Two with Lenny B.
And I am resurrected. Just as you
Turn off the hackneyed Strauss,
I come alive. The foot is firmly in the other shoe!

And don't forget, those Strauss boys
Weren't all Waltz Kings. Tune your ear…
Do you remember Rosenkavalier?
Da-da-dee…I play it in my head.
Music is memory, last thing to go,
And never dead.

So, could you write a poem if you'd forgotten
That those damn Strauss's made you feel so rotten?
And would you have been Poet Laureate
If you had cleared your slate? The answer: Nyet!

Then if Today is glorious, why, seize it!
You never know when it might come in handy
But as for me, the past, I just deep-freeze it,
To defrost, and be savored like fine brandy.

The Plath Untaken

If Sylvia
Had gone a different route,
Put a loaf in the oven
Instead.
What might she have become?

An aging icon, outliving
And out-reading Ted?
Would she be preserving her past,
Dissecting her history
From a new perspective?

If she'd had one good woman friend...
Did she have any?
To pull her back to reality,
Remind her of her two beautiful children,
And a future.
How well she could have set that torture
To verse, examine it minutely.
The well would not run dry.

Become a guru to young poets…
(She might hate that if they were young
And beautiful…)
Honorary degrees would
Soften the blow
Of growing old.
She would become Poet Laureate,
Yes, and watch the children grow,
Knowing their rich mix of genes,
How could she let them go?
What depth of desperation,
To let the future continue
Without you.

Or did she think
It was the thing that
Women poets do?

Anne Frank

We were born three months apart.
How easily
We could have been each other.

A quirk of fate?
For every theory there's a flaw,
A name.
If my Grandparents
Hadn't left a generation sooner
Our fates may well
Have been the same.

She came so close to living on,
I think of Anne,
Her short life, mine so long.

She should have had a world
Filled with love and laughter,
A story that deserved Forever After.

Her grandchildren would fascinate her now,
Accomplishments that followed in her line.
I know it, that's the way it is with mine.
How many Anne-alikes came through?
How many others gone, we never knew.

Obituary, the Last of the Beguines
Marcella Pattyn, May 30, 2013, age 92

Now we know who the last of them was,
But we still don't know
Who Began the Beguines.

It ended after 800 years of goodness,
A way of religion unknown to man…they were all
women.
Needing to take no vows of obedience
Or poverty…a vow of chastity was voluntary
And they might leave to marry.
They could own property and some were wealthy,
But they were classless.

Did they know they were Feminists?
Of course not.
They tended the sick, cared for the poor,
Prayed for the dying.
Lived in their own communes.

Marcella, nearly blind, spent her days
Knitting, weaving, making dolls to sell to tourists,
She played the organ in Church
And the banjo and accordion to the sick…
She didn't know she was a Music Therapist.
But in her Beguinage in Ghent, built in 1238,
She ended her life. Ended the Beguines.

Eight hundred years of peace.
The world has a lot to learn.

Paradise Lost

Southern Iraq 2004

The Garden of Eden is dead.
Parched and flyblown,
Dingy sheep, chewing on the few surviving
Tufts of grass, do not safely graze.
Eden is now a bleak morass
Seen through a dusty haze.

The Tree of Knowledge,
Of Good and Evil,
Is lifeless.
No apples, no temptation,
No snake...is this the work of the Devil?

Untended, forgotten history,
No tourists questioning its mystery.
Did anyone think Paradise
Would last forever?

Picasso's Doves

Another Season to make merry.
Another dove.
But has this symbol of hope,
This bird of Peace,
Become passé?
Unthinkable,
Picasso a cliché.

The world is wearied, wary,
Something unsettled in the air.
And anyone can see,
The gentle dove
Has done us no more good
Than prayer.

Stonehenge, the Latest Theory

Before there was a word for it,
No less an Art or Science,
The ancients gathered at Stonehenge
To form a strange alliance.

They'd heard some stones had ringing tones,
And so went off to find them,
Then schlepped them back to Salisbury Plain
And more or less aligned them.

They banged their gongs and onged their chants,
And gathered up a few sticks,
And what they heard, no man nor nerd
Could know would be Acoustics.

And what a beat they improvised,
(Though limited their menu,)
Oblivious that they'd devised
The first Rock Music venue.

For Christopher Springthorpe, June 2014

And Suddenly He Sings

Our silent swan
Opens up his throat
And there, in disbelief
We are enthralled with every note.

A rich, deep bodied baritone…
And not just that, it's liede that he sings.
His father plays, he stands alone
With no theatricality, an athletic
Seventeen year old in jeans,
Who sings in German
Schubert would have understood,
While we are choking back the tears.

This miracle before our ears…
Yes, sometimes life is good.

For Nicholas Springthorpe, August 2014

Peeling Apples, Welwyn

An Indian Summer afternoon,
Sitting under a tree
In Karen's garden
With a huge basket of windfalls
To peel, core, remove worms
And cut up for applesauce.

Seven year old Christopher abandons
Kicking his football and watches with interest.
"Grandma, can I have a go?"
He is impatient to try his hand at it.

I give him the parer and an apple,
Correct his first attempt.
He concentrates and gets the hang
Of it quite quickly
I show him a virtuoso turn,
Getting the whole peel off in
One continuous twirl.
He marvels and can't wait to try again.

We sit in the sun, he peeling,
Me performing the surgery,
Cutting and slicing until
The huge saucepan is filled to the brim.

The scent is sweet. The moment is indelible.

Blame it on Berlioz

You walked into my life
With your Berlioz records
Sixty years ago,
Convinced that he was one of the
Great under-recognized composers.

Romeo and Juliette did it for me.

I thought you were a man of vision
And maybe we could see the future together.

We have.
And Berlioz has come a long way, too.

Addenda: In the interim I have come to prefer Prokofiev's version, but it's too late now!

Mixed Marriage

We have a mixed marriage,
Sans Bible or icon or joss stick…
One of us is an Atheist,
The other an Agnostic.

We're fervent and observant,
Except, that here's the hitch:
After fifty years
We've forgotten who is which.

Marriage á la Mode

Atop the cake
Stand side by side,
A charming pair
Of Bride and Bride.

And somewhere there's
A honeymoon
Suite welcoming
A groom and groom.

The only problem I foresee
Of incompatibility,
Relates to towels…
And here's the hitch:

Which "His" is whose?
Whose "Hers" is which?

A Chorus to St. Thesaurus

The Road to Oblivion
Is paved with writer's blocks,
With parallelepipidons of insignificance
And poppycocks.

I am brinkling at the doorway to Oblitery,
A venerable person of extinction,
The very essence of built-in obsolescence,
Whose sole function is to punch in
At that Great Big Lit'ry luncheon in the Sky,
And dance a gavroche with Anonymous Bosch,
Thigh to thigh.

My passport and my visa's inked
With authorized indifference
By a faceless stupornumery, who
To my maternal shame
Stamps in: "Whatsername."

No need for me the nom de plume,
My nom's void as an empty tomb,
My plume has molted, quill is blunt,
The technique's merely peck and hunt.
Laureate of the White Page,
Recipient of the sow's purse,
Keeping a low profile and cancelled Poetic License.

Worse, I rummage through old phrases,
Toss them in a pail I'll flim-flame at some
Mumble Jumble sale, to help feed flabby minds
With flummoxed words too meager
For a flock of undernourished Myna birds.
Indelible and gullible
Right down to the last syllable.

Some deity in wisdom and sobriety,
Has cancelled my subscription to Society.
Oh, the Schaden-freude blooms so gloomously.
That slender volume…will it come prehumously?
If so, I know begrundiously I'd thank it,
While thumbling my Obscurity blanket.

Writers Bloc

I want to break into jail.
How else will I ever have time
To write all day uninterrupted...
Unfortunately that's not a crime.

Stealing...I have no more storage,
And murder's not my kind of fun.
I'm too tired for crimes of grand passion,
And won't be caught dead with a gun.

I'd find inside trading degrading,
And forgery's out, with my scrawl,
I'm sure I'd go blank if I held up a bank,
And don't see myself in a brawl.

I'm lacking the talent for hacking,
And smuggling's a struggling test,
But I think there's one thing I've a knack in,
Where I'm at my best...I'll PROTEST!!!

Then surely they'll come and arrest me,
And throw me right into the clink,
And no one will dare to contest me,
So I'll have months to write and to think.

My dream: no more cooking or housework,
No meetings, no shopping, no phone
I've paid all my taxes and answered my faxes
Now I'll have a cell of my own.

Just a wee little nest and my iPad
And I'll toss off a novel or two,
It's a Writers Retreat and it's my pad,
So who needs a room with a view!

Let's just hope I don't have a savior,
Who misses my domestic skill.
And gets me out on good behavior…
Then I'll really be ready to kill.

Wits End

When we were young
Our witticisms bounced
Off each other.
Our badinage like
Feathered shuttlecocks
Flew back and forth...
And what's more,
Were retrievable.

Bon mots,
Like bon-bons to be
Savored again and again.
A language of our own,
Our frame of reference,
Gilded and baroque.
We always got the other's joke.

But they have flown.
We're old now,
A few less feathers...
(our boas are constricted,
We might have said, God help us)
Our mots vanish instantly
Into the ether,
Melted into clouds.
And we say "What?"
A lot.

Badinage...could that translate to:
"Bad in age"?
Dommage!

Perhaps when we arrive
Up There...in Jewish Athiests Heaven...
No God, but full of resuscitated wags,
Wits, word teasers, jesters, manic impressives,
Nudging for seats around that big Algonquin.
Table in the sky,

With angels serving
Zabar's nova on H&H bagels,
And Harpo and Myor Rosen strumming arpeggios,
You, my Other Half,
And I, the Other Laugh,
Will join up at the hip
Replacement
And what's left of us
Refit into one whole
Born again Wit...

Hallelujah!!

For Betsy Gehman on her 90th birthday, 2013

A Ship Too Far

Remember those striving years, Sisters and Brothers,
When the way of the world was: Out-do unto Others?
Who owned the most art, took the ultimate trip...
We were caught in a frenzy of One Up-man-ship.

Now we're old and that ship's a lot like Titanic,
Our cruises are tamer, there's no buying panic.
Old coots are now shooting straight from the (new) hip,
And the daily obits supply One Down-man-ship.

River Stones on the Upsalquitch

These stones in their infinite variety
Bring out the scavenger in us,
Our inner child.
Unlimited possibilities
When the imagination runs wild..
Hearts, cigars, monsters and monograms,
A wedge of cheese, looked at another way,
A sail. Hidden treasures, objets trouvée,
Tossed carelessly…a boot, a whale.
Tumbled by harsh winter's flow,
Shaped by millennia of ice and snow.
Colors, the spectrum of blacks and whites
To pinks and terra cottas, and combinations
Of them all. "Rosetta Stones" with mysterious
scratchings,
Gift-wrapped stones with white stripes across them
In geometry no school could teach.
Now all loosely assembled on the beach
Beneath our feet.
So, which will be the chosen few
To leave the Upsalquitch, and be transported
To a life of leisure, to start
New lives as Works of Art.
Until we return next year to add a sequel.
These are mementos
That no tourist shop could ever equal.

For Joan and Livy Parsons, July 2013

My Cup Runneth Over
(and Staineth the Tablecloth)

My glass was half empty,
Until I was thrilled
To learn the good news:
It was really half filled!

And just as I found
I was living in clover,
It surged to the brim,
And the damn thing ran over.

So here, with my luck,
I am stuck in the mud...
Is there no middle ground
That's between drought and flood?

This eternal dilemma
Has always plagued man.
So I'll pass on the glass
And drink straight from the can.

At the Wallace Collection of Clocks

Here, if you will,
Is Tempus standing still.
Not fugiting or fidgeting,
Or swooping for the kill.

Merely in a suspended state,
Inanimate,
With nothing else to do.

Let's match its mode,
Catch up with déjà vu.

STOP ALL THE CLOCKS!!
Perhaps turn back a few.
A decade wouldn't go amiss,
Or even better, two.

Gladly return those ticks and tocks
We barely listened to.
And if we can't do that,
At least then stay
Just where we are today.

And oh, forget about the chimes…
They're even more cliché than rhymes.

Waiting Room

Here's how I know I'm old:
Our doctor (who we love), is a Geriatrician
And though
The inside of my head
Is not yet quite brain dead,
I am vaguely depressed
In her waiting room,
With the slow and steady flow
Of Frank Sinatra...or today,
Hooray! It's Doris Day.

These ballads are meant to remind us
Of our Prime Times, our best years,
With their Tin Pan Alley sentiments.
But now they seem so stale,
Like has-beens...which they are.
Those singers are all dead,
And we're still here.
Is that supposed to bolster us with cheer?

If you want dead,
How about Good and Dead, instead.
A touch of Mozart, Bach.
They've stood up well in time,
And long run's what we're here for.

Or while we're waiting for longevity,
Montiverdi's even older, and the spice
Of life that might transport us to
The waiting room of Paradise.

The New Old Age

What do you call an old Codger that's politically correct?
How to address a Geezer with appropriate respect?
Just because we're olden
We're not fooled by that word "Golden,"
So avoid the subject with benign neglect.

If we're elderly, don't say it, because it's not polite.
"Crones" and "Fossils" are the way to turn our hair white overnight.
So here's a plan ahora, he's Senior, and I'm Seniora,
And I think Si, Si, we might have got it right!

Olé!

Read My Lips

I'm 80
And I still wear lipstick.
Redder than ever this year.

It says:
"Listen, I'm still here."
This invisible face,
These indelible lips,
Still have something to say.

Watch this space!

The Poem I Cannot Quite Write to My Daughters

With the millions of words
That are there for the taking,
I lack all the skills that it takes
For the making
Of one perfect verse…
Or preferably two
That captures the essence of each of you,
That even hints of the all embracing
Depth of my love, and since time is racing,
Perhaps this memo will have to do
In the meantime, as an I.O.U.

Passing Through

Old age
Is just a stage
You're going through.
The pity is,
That when it's over,
So are you.

Self-Assessment on My 86th Birthday

The grains of ambition
Have drained through the sieve.
Too old to die young,
So I might as well live.

And while I'm about it,
Before the Long Rest,
It makes sense to savor
What's left of the zest.

ACKNOWLEDGMENTS

"Viola d'Amore" and "Connoisseur" appeared in *Faber Book of Blue Verse*, Faber and Faber, and also *Making Love to Marilyn*, Viking. "Mother Funk" appeared in *In the Gold of Flesh*, Women's Press. "Side Effects" in *Lighten Up*, Meadowbrook Press. Others have appeared in *Light Years, Bits Press, SHE Magazine, Cosmopolitan, The Spectator, The New Statesman, Light Quarterly, Wall Street Journal*.

AND MY THANKS TO

This book would never have happened without the gentle prodding, editorial wizardry and wit of my daughter Elissa; My husband, Fred's constant support and undying enthusiasm; Monika Beisner's magical talent and generosity for the use of the cover picture; My old pal, Lawrence Holofcener's offering me a seat between his famous "Allies"; Nancy Mato's beautiful friendship and All Seeing Eye; Geraldine Aikman's many long range skills; Norman Sunshine's first reading and encouragement, and the Society of the Four Arts Sculpture Garden.

Joan Van Poznak was born in New York. After studying at Juilliard Preparatory School, she spent two magical summers as a student at Tanglewood, attended the Neighborhood Playhouse School of Theater, and is still recovering from Modern dance classes with Martha Graham.

Soon after, she made her operatic debut and farewell performance simultaneously (as Mozart's " Bastienne") in one dazzling evening, then accidentally fell in to pop group singing, thinking she was auditioning for yet another madrigal ensemble.

Joan worked through the Golden Age of live black and white TV, backing such performers as Kate Smith (she was a Katydid), Lena Horne, Louis Armstrong, Perry Como and Ella Fitzgerald, before retiring to Connecticut as the wife of a surgeon and the mother of two wonderful daughters. They moved to London in 1974, where she became a longstanding (and sitting) member of the London Symphony Chorus, and have divided their time between West Palm Beach and London ever since. Along the way they acquired two talented grandsons.